This is Death, Love, Life

Dedication

To Lilly,
For being my rock and my place of refuge in the
most tumultuous of times.

To Owen,
For showing me what it truly means to be strong.

To Deborah Walling,
For encouraging me to write.

To Jacob,
Who I can always go to write with, to scheme with,
and to laugh with.

To Matthew and Ronan,
My brothers without whom I would be lost.

To you, the reader
If not for your, my poetry would be meaningless. So,
thank you for taking the time to even open this book,
and thank you for supporting me in my writing.

For more poetry by Travis Liebert:

Follow my Social Media:

Instagram - @travisliebert
Tumblr - @travisliebert
Facebook.com/authortravisliebert
Twitter - @travisliebert

Visit my website: alltheseinkspots.com

Find my other books on Amazon:

Perchance to Dream (Book 2 of *The Shattered Verses*)
Everything in Between (Book 3 of *The Shattered Verses*)
The Shattered Verses Bundle

There is life
And there is death
And sometimes
If we're lucky
A little love in between

Death

Regardless of my futile actions no happiness ensued,
And thus I had to ask myself "whatever shall I do?"
And so I found a somber mask and painted it with a smile,
And put it on in hopes that it would last me for a while.
But as time advanced the face I wore began to crack and fade,
Until the countenance it bore no happiness portrayed.
And all t'was left was fear and guilt and lies and icy sin,
That glared from out the mirror with a melancholy grin,
That watched as I lay 'wake at night regretting things long past,
That stood like king atop the pile of regrets I had amassed,
That gripped my sodden heart with all the strength that I'd long lost,
That edged me toward lines that I did not want nor dare to cross.
Now sadness is all I care to feel within my hollow frame,
I know I must do something to ease this aching pain,
And so I'll wistfully remove that somber mask again,
And tear away the sadness with a bullet through my brain.

   -Mask

We wage wars inside our minds
Silent fights behind our eyes
Maimed by words unkindly said
Tamed by our prescription meds
But trudging on with all our might
We veterans of silent fights
Hope that we'll see better days
As long as we attempt to stay
Alive

   -*Alive*

Depression
That foul beast
Which scuttles out
From within my psyche
And no exterminator
No therapy
No drugs
Can kill it
So I only hope
To scare it
To terrify it
To chase it
Back into whatever
Putrid hole
From which it clambered
And hope it never realizes
That it's the real monster
And I'm the one
That's scared
          -Depression

There are days I am sick
So sick in the head
When I ask the clock why it continues to tick
And proclaim without shame that I'd rather be dead
When my heart feels numb and my mind feels thick
And my limbs feel fashioned from lead
So I bide and I wait and I watch for the trick
For the trick to extinguish my dread
And the whole time I hope that my death might come
quick
Come quick as I lie in my bed
　　-There Are Days I Am Sick

One day I told myself
Maybe I should die
After all, the world is sad
So sad that I might cry
So I climbed up on the roof
And looked down upon the yard
But when I looked upon ground
The ground looked mighty hard
So I climbed down from the roof
And settled for a rope
But the rope was mighty rough
And it would surely chafe my throat
So I took my father's gun
And put it to my head
But the gun was mighty cold
And though I wished that I was dead
It was cold upon my temple
Too cold to tolerate
So I put the gun away
And chose to live another day
-I Chose to Live another Day

Ghosts exist
They wander out of funeral homes
And haunt cemeteries
Visiting the same grave
Over and over and over
Leaving flowers
And prayers
Just hoping to feel alive once again
        -Hoping to Feel Alive

Cancer of the mind.
That's what depression is.
It's my mind
turning against itself.
It's part of me.
There is no distinction
between it and me.
I don't know
who I am
without it.
There is no surgery
To cut out this tumor.
And just like cancer,
I'm slowly killing myself.
                -Cancer

Shaky breath within thy chest,
The icy tendrils snare.
Trapped between thine woeful sobs,
And achings of despair.
Oh patiently pale Death shall wait,
A fate one can't ignore.
And though thee mortals may win battles,
Death shall always win the war.
For pale Death has always been,
And Death shall always be.
Looming gloomy in the future,
Though at first so distantly.
But as the weary years progress,
And age invades thine eyes,
Death's pale form shall take its shape,
And impending closure rise.
And though thou may see Death's true frame,
And how thine end ensues,
Grievously there's no escape,
Tis a fate one can't refuse.
And so it seems all thee can do,
Is wistfully trudge on,
And wait for Death as he for us,
At sunset thereupon.
        -Pale Death

Depression isn't wanting to
Die
It's simply not wanting to
Live
There are no good days to die
But there are bad days to live
When the skies are gray
The sun isn't gone
It's merely obscured
But when every day is gray
There might as well be
No sun at all
-When Every Day is Gray

We fear change.
We fear what it represents
Change is an inescapable
Aspect of the flux of life.
It is the physical
Incarnation of the unknown.
And the unknown
Is utterly horrifying.
        -Change

Vincent van Gogh
You genius of the Netherlands
With broken mind yet steady hand
Doing everything he can
To let the whole world know
The love you have despite your woe
And how you wished they'd love you so
A love that you would never know
So haunted by your pain and strife
In that wretched field you took your life
Those people who ignored your cries
Now dress in black and dry their eyes
They only love you once you've died
        -They Only Love You Once You've Died

Nobody loves me
And I cannot love myself
Perhaps I'm simply ill
And illness can be helped
But that's not the way it feels
That's not the way it seems
I'll say farewell to this loveless world
And then I'll take my leave
      -I'll Take My Leave

God must be old.
Terribly old.
His every movement a struggle.
Never still.
Always trembling.
Because the priest tells me
that my life
is in the hands of god.
And I've always lived
Such a shaky life.

-God Must Be Old

Cigarette burns on my favorite shirt
Inhaling the smoke and exhaling the hurt
Trying to clear the tears away
While driving one hundred and ten

Thinking about how I'll always be lonely
And knowing that she'll never want me
I stray to the dark parts of my mind
While chasing it down with gin

And I wonder if I'll ever feel right
If I could somehow open my eyes to the light
If I may one day be able to see
Something to take me away from the pain

But, the pain, I just can't ignore it
So I press the pedal and floor it
Hoping that once I'm wrapped around a tree
I won't be so bent out of shape

And my life, it flashes before me
In the smoke, it's such a sad story
A story that is so sad
I decide I don't want to see the end quite yet
        -Cigarette Burns

Ever since we lost you
I feel like I've been lost too
My soul doesn't shine
Quite like it used to
It seems like I'm dying
I'm not sure if I'll pull through
     -*My Soul Doesn't Shine*

Drowning tears with whiskey
Drowning out sobs with music
Smothering mourning with cigarette smoke
Even as we lived
We died

-Even as We Lived

In our times and trials
We each must walk a path,
Through emptiness and pain,
In hopes of something that will last.
In hopes that we can fill our void,
If only for a moment,
And feel a grain of happiness,
But alas I must forgo it.

For I am a man of solemn disposition,
Searching, searching, searching
For a cure to my condition.
In my dreams I see a man
Who stands as if fulfilled,
But such are dreams as they can never be fulfilled.

And so I'll keep on walking,
For fear of dwelling on my past,
With shoulders bowed
And furrowed brow
In hopes of something that will last.
                -Something That Will Last

The sunlight hurts my eyes
I choke on the summer breeze
I've grown tired of this world
Perhaps the world is tired of me
        -Tired

I wash away my sorrows with whiskey, beer, and rum
Alcohol's a chaser for every wrong thing that I've
done
And though it may not make the familiar ache abate
and quit
It allows my sorry soul to stop, forgive, forget
But only for a moment for the drunken numbness is
fleeting
And thus I find this process to be one I keep
repeating
I wake up every morning with a drumming in my
brain
Such drumming is but nothing compared to other
pain
The pain of my mistakes, lost lives, and broken hearts
The stain of my transgressions that tear my soul
apart
And though I know I may one day find some hope
again

For now, I'll simply settle down and drown myself in
gin

  -Sorrow's Chaser

I think mental illness
is to be a little too
in touch with reality.
To strip away
the suspension of disbelief
that makes life
just barely
bearable

-Barely Bearable

I'm a drug addict.
I'm addicted to my antidepressants.
I'm addicted
to not being sad.
I'll do anything
to get my fix
of stability.

-I'm a Drug Addict

Tonight, poor Johnny sits at home
Still in his funeral clothes
Staring blankly at the wall
And wallowing in his woes

He grasps a silver flask
And lifting it to his lips
Assumes his nightly task
Of drinking with the God of Loneliness

Tonight, Harry lies outside
Where the grass is cold and wet
Staring sadly at the stars
And trying to forget

He perceives the cosmic patterns
And pointing at the abyss
He then begins with Saturn
Tracing the God of Loneliness

Tonight, Marie is in her room
Where she sobs the silence away
Meditating on her loss
And drowning in dismay

She lies there all night long
Wishing she didn't exist
And turning on her saddest song
Sings with the God of Loneliness

Tonight, old George sits by himself
At a table he had set for two
And realizes that it's something
He no longer has to do

He wearily removes the extra wares
Wishing he could give her one last kiss
Then settles back into his chair
And feasts with the God of Loneliness

Tonight, Sarah stands inside a room
That's been painted baby blue
While her husband works away from home
Doing all that he can do

To forget the dusty crib whereby
Sarah stands and still persists
In cooing out a lullaby
Serenading the God of Loneliness

Tonight, the poet writes on his own
A ballad of heartbreak and sadness
His muse is born from being too long alone
His muse is the God of Madness.
          -The God of Loneliness

Depression
is having a heart
that constantly pumps sadness
through your veins
and desperately wanting
that heart to stop.
        -*Sad Blood*

If I am to be a prince
Let me be Hamlet
If I am to be a king
Let me be Oedipus
If I am to be a messiah
Let me be Jesus
I was born for tragic ends
I am a star
A firework
The Space Shuttle Challenger
I rise to new heights
And burn
Ever so brightly
Leaving spots in your vision
That can't be
Blinked away
So
If I am to burn
Let me burn

-Let Me Burn

I sat down by the River Styx
And found the sound of all my woes
The babble of the River Styx
Did within itself enclose
I saw the world in darker hues
Blacks and grays and somber blues
A sorry sight so sad and bitter
That forced me then to reconsider
Whether life was worth the effort
Or worth the time and work I give
That made me think it would be better
If I should die rather than live
  -The River Styx

If I could wish upon a star
Upon the light that's come so far
And traveled all this way until
I bend the light unto my will
And tell to it my wants and whims
Whispering my hopeful hymns
Then gazing up I thus intone
"Please don't let me be alone."
            -Upon a Star

We venture out into the world
And assume our shameful daily task
Of fearing what our peers might think
And putting on a public mask
Smothering our private passions
Behind our masks we suffocate
And watch as others do the same
Letting their dreams asphyxiate
    -Asphyxiation

I was told that writing,
That poetry,
Was career suicide
That my intellect
Was suited for
Med School
Law School
Engineering
They told me that
Rather than kill my career
I should kill myself
-Career Suicide

I remember that foul morning
When they interrupted class
And in a voice replete with mourning
Said you were never coming back
I stood out in the hallway
And watched our English teacher cry
We ate in silence that day
We never thought you'd die
It always is so horrid
The passing of a youth
So depressing, sad, and morbid
A cruel and somber truth
I can't believe you're gone
You've left wounds I'll never mend
But I'll bear my scars and continue on
Rest in peace my friend
            -Rest in Peace My Friend

Why'd you have to go?
It's not your fault, I know.
But no matter how hard I try,
Or how much I seek to live,
I can never fill the void you left,
Or make up for the life you never got to give.
There was so much left for you to do.
So many places you could go.
I don't know how to live for two.
I can barely live for myself, you know?
But I promise I'll keep trying.
I'll carry you in my soul.
I'll live for you my brother.
But how I miss you so.
I wish you were here my friend.
I wish you were with me O.
        -*Why'd You Have to Go*

I always thought I couldn't be
Loved
Until I loved myself
And I couldn't love myself
Until I believed I could be loved
I know love is never straightforward
But no one ever told me it was a fucking
Paradox
    -Love is a Paradox

We stumble onward, forward, advancing through the passing years
Ardent for what is to come, ignorant to such horrors that the future bears
For in the eyes of sanguine youth the future seems to burn so bright
And yet as time reveals the truth so it diminishes the light
And as we trudge beyond the present the mass of time shall weigh us down
Bending, bowing, sagging sorry backs until we are blind but to the ground
And still we foolheartedly continue on, never averting our eyes
Hoping, striving, plodding on, we comfort ourselves with lies
We mutter to ourselves that the night is always darkest before dawn
And convince our beaten bodies that we should still continue on
We dare not close our eyes for fear of missing morning sun's first ray
Knowing in our heart of hearts that, for us, the sun is always half a world away

-Distant Dawn

God has alzheimer's disease
Why else would he have forgotten me?
-God Has Alzheimer's

We're all sinners in the end
We can't begin again
My heart aches for a world long lost
They say a war is on the way
It could happen any day
And we can't presume to know the cost
All I know is that I'm scared
All I know is that I'm sad
Trapped in a world gone mad
I wish somebody cared
I wish that we could change
But it seems we're all the same
We're all sinners in the end
We can't begin again
I don't believe in God
I don't believe in heaven
But I'm still afraid to die
So I stop to pray and cry
As I look up to the empty sky
And crouched down on my knees
I beseech 'please oh please,'
'Can you teach us how to love again?'
            -We're All Sinners in the End

Love

This is not poetry
She was poetry
To encapsulate her
To trap her
To confine her to words
Is impossible
And quite frankly
Ridiculous
Nonetheless
I try

-This is Not Poetry

She is different
Which is dumb to say
Everyone's different
But she's different
In the way I'm different
And for that
I love her
-She is Different

Heaven
Is when I'm with
You
Hell
Is all the time
In between
-Heaven and Hell

If love is a
Prison
Then I plead
Guilty
And ask only that I
Serve a life sentence
-I Plead Guilty

She
Just She
That's all I can say
For no verse can epitomize her
Nothing can ever amount to her image
That leaps forth in my mind
When I mutter her name
So all I say is
She

-She

You are the fullest moon on the darkest night
Guiding me with supple light
And though you may be far away
I promise that some future day
Hopefully it will be soon
I'll be the one to catch the moon
    -I'll be the One to Catch the Moon

When I'm with you I always find
Our hearts and souls are intertwined
Silent Words from mind to mind
As I stare into your eyes
Turquoise eyes with crystal depth
A loving gaze that steals my breath
I pull you tight into my chest
And never let you go
            -Never Let You Go

Perhaps the edges of our broken hearts
Don't quite fit together
But I'm willing to whittle myself away
Carving at my heart all day
Until it fits
Beside your heart
Where it will never come apart
So that I may be
With you
    -Our Broken Hearts

A rose
Yes
She was a rose
A rose who wilted
Waiting for one
Who dared to grasp
Her thorns
-A Rose

Words
Were not enough
To express my feelings for you
So I turned to poetry
Fuck
I'm either a bad poet
Or my feelings for you
Are too complex
To ever be confined
To words
Or paper
Or ink
Or even poetry
        -*Words*

My happiness knows no bounds
Whenever she comes around
Her eyes and smile both resound
With my soul wherein I've found
A realization so profound
I fill with joy that knows no bounds
Because I'm in love
So deep in love I hope to drown
        -I Hope to Drown

She was beautiful when she slept
But that beauty
Paled in comparison
To her dazzling blue eyes
And sleepy voice
And tousled hair
When she awoke and said
"I love you"
>   *-When She Slept*

I want to hold her in my arms
Beneath the moon and all the stars
I wish to stare into her eyes
As we lie beneath the spangled sky
I'll pull her tight into my chest
And feel her heartbeat through her breast
And as we lie, just her and me
I'll have found true ecstasy
-Beneath the Spangled Sky

She lit a fire
In my heart
And her kisses
Stoke the flames
   -She Lit a Fire

You did not take a piece of my heart
When you left
You didn't take it
Because I gave it to you
It's yours to have
Yours to keep
Yours to carry with you forever
With or without me
        -*Yours to Keep*

She says my name
And I fall in love
All over again
        -All Over Again

rless
When she is with me
The impossible
Suddenly becomes possible
When she is mine
The world is mine as well
   -The World is Mine

What a beautiful home
I've found in your heart
   -She Has a Beautiful Heart

As I bid the day adieu
And the dark begins to beckon
I think about what I know to be true
I know that God is not in Heaven
And the world is all askew
I know that life is one big question
And I don't know what to do
I know I'm terrified of depression
And I get scared when I'm feeling blue
So I'll hold tight to you
And never let you go
        -I'll Hold Tight to You

Won't you come hold me
Won't you come help me
I'm at the mercy of my mind
And I'm not fine
So won't you come hold me
Wrap your arms around my body
Tell me that I'm yours
And tell me that you're mine
Encircled by your arms
I just might feel fine
        -Won't You Come Hold Me

As long as you love me
Nothing can stop me
You are my muse
So kiss me soft
Cover my neck in your tattoos
Hold me tight
Love me fast
My fate is sealed
The die is cast
I am forever yours
-I am Forever Yours

Life

There are no good days to die
But there are bad days
To live

I live for those days
I live
To die

I live
To burn
To cry

But more than that
More importantly
I live

   -I Live

I don't believe in miracles
But I do believe
That sometimes
On a good day
When the wind is in the right direction
And your heart is in the right place
And you're willing to look
To really look
You'll see that
The impossible does happen
And those impossible things
Seem a lot like miracles
-Miracles

Humans
Are not candles
They don't burn out
They get tired
When a candle sputters out
It's done
Forever
Humans are never done
We don't sputter out
Not if we don't let ourselves
We are never truly done
-We Are Never Truly Done

So it goes in human life
Filled with hope and filled with strife
We tend to always look behind
But claim to walk ahead

And so we crane our necks around
Shuffling across the ground
Focused only on what was
And not on what might be

Release the tension in your spine
And in your neck and in your mind
And look ahead where you might find
The future that you need
   -The Future that You Need

)urself
And love the world
And don't apologize
For who you are
Sing your songs
Draw your art
Write your poems
Passion
Is never a sin

-Passion is Never a Sin

Don't be afraid to be crazy
Anyone who ever did anything was
Crazy
You have to break your mind
Before you break the mold
So be impulsive
Let loose
You'd be crazy not to
      -Be Crazy

Love in all things.
All you think.
All you say.
All you do.
Do not fear
The pursuit of love.
Be it a person.
Be it a career.
Do not fear
What is looked
Down upon.
Society waits to
Be disturbed.
But if you must
Disturb it
Do so with love.

-Love in All Things

I chose to walk a different path
And thus strayed from the crowd
And when I dared to look around
I found myself alone
But I also found without the crowd
And its trite insipid drone
I had room to spread my wings
And also room to grow
      -Room to Grow

My heart
my old heart
No matter how battered or beaten or bruised
Or badly abused
How scarred and how marred
How badly tattooed
In black and in blue
It continues to beat
To pulse and repeat
The rhythm by which
Through thin and through thick
It's continued to tick
And carry my dreams-
My hopes and my schemes
Through chuckles and sobs
It continues to throb
This old heart is tougher than it seems
  -My Old Heart

Everyone dies
But not everyone lives
You can't avoid death
So don't avoid life
Either
Love completely
Live fully
Die happy
    -Live Fully

The world is yours.
Yours to rule.
Yours to live
a life that's full.
Yours to hope.
Yours to dream.
Yours to write to sing to scheme.
So free yourself
from the chains of fear.
The world is yours.
The world is here.

-The World is Here

One day we will die
We will drift off to sleep
Lulled from life by the sea
Born into rest for eternity
But for now we're alive
And for now we are young
So although we might die
And our lovers might cry
Let's enjoy one more trip around the sun
    -One More Trip

I wish to live
To live brightly
To live strongly
To live fully
So fully that my chest
Will continue to rise
And fall
In my casket
And Death will raise his hand
And ask permission to take me
        -Death Will Ask Permission

Writing is like shouting
Into the void
The void is dark
The void is scary
But shout loud
And shout clear
And soon enough
Someone will hear
      -Writing is Like Shouting

Write
Write your love
And write your fear
And write it all out crystal clear
So you can then reread your verse
Traverse a written universe
Enshrined inside your poignant words
It matters not how long or terse
Your pensive prose will one day birth
Progeny of love and fear
Depicted candid and sincere
Thus you may know what's in your soul
Know it all and know it whole
So all that peer upon your prose
And stop to probe what you compose
And forgo all they know
Can freely read beyond the ink
And comprehend what poets think
And thus they may then understand
The feelings of an unknown man
And learn to love all unknown men
Regardless of their speech or skin
And begin to mend the world again
To quell the swells of spite and sin
And defend against spells of despair
Resolving resentment here and there
Resolved because you dared to bare
Your soul which through your prose was shared
And swear to make the world aware
Of how to love and how to care
And ensure that none become ensnared
In all the hate we must beware

Through motley words and rhymes declared
In pedantic prose you've pruned and pared
With all your will withheld within
Conveyed through heart and mind and pen
        -Write it Out

Everybody wants to be
Somebody
Nobody is willing to be
Themselves
    -Somebody

I only want to be kind
To love
To care
If compassion is weakness
Then I strive to be the weakest of them all
     -I Want to be Kind

It's okay to be different
The world may be puzzling
But it's not a puzzle
And not everyone is meant to fit in
Be yourself
Live your life
It's yours to live
-The World is not a Puzzle

We strive onward, onward, onward,
And hold our hopes within.
Searching for all the world offers,
And seeking out the strength of better men.

Thus we tiptoe forward,
A game of inches, not of feet,
Trying to be better men,
Thus we hopefully repeat:

"Dear strength, dear hope, dear honor,
Dear all that is within me,
How shall I become a man,
Lacking vice and hate and envy?"

For what makes up a man
But the sum of his own past?
So make good choices, thoughts and actions,
And become a man whose life will last.

Will last in the hearts and minds of others,
In their actions and their deeds,
In their hopes and aspirations,
And inspire them to sing:

"Dear strength, dear hope, dear honor,
Dear all that is within me,
How shall I become a man,
Lacking vice and hate and envy?"
        -*We Strive Onward*

People always say
"Fight the good fight"
What they really mean is
"Fight"
"Just Fight"
Because a fight is a struggle
There's no such thing
As a good struggle
So just struggle
But struggle well
　　　　-Struggle Well

Hope against hope
Hope against fate
Hope against your fears and fancies
Hope until you fully can't see
All the things that almost could be
And all the things that almost would be
So all you know is what you should be
And thus you wait and concentrate
On your future and your fate
And surely then you can create
A life without the leaden weight
Of fears by which you hesitate
You'll find you can now extricate
Yourself from your old stagnant state
A life in which you'd suffocate
And seek the life that must await
Behind the blinds of future dates
Where you are free to cultivate
A world that you can love
        -*Hope*

Those who rave,
the mad,
who crave the impossible,
are those who love
life most.
Love it so much
they choose to live
shockingly,
impossibly,
blindingly
fast,
and so the good,
the mad,
die young.

-The Good, The Mad

Keep moving forward
Even if you must
Walk on eggshells
And if your feet fall heavy
Or you can't help but tread
With hasty gait
No matter
No matter
After all
You can't make an omelette
Without breaking
Some eggs
-Keep Moving Forward

We are not moths
Drawn to a flame.
Rather,
We are whales
Drifting aimlessly
Beneath the waves,
And the light we see
Is the open air
Above.
And though we
Are born for water,
If we don't reach
That light, we will
Drown.

-Drifting Aimlessly

Loving yourself
Isn't vanity.
It's okay to love
Yourself.
As long as you
Love others
In the process.
      -Love Yourself

On the Fourth of July
Families don't
Go outside
And light candles.
They don't gather round
And gasp in awe
As a candle
Flickers in the wind
For hours.
It's not about
How long you burn,
But how bright.
So don't just burn.
Burn brightly.
-Burn Brightly

This is for my friends
I am with you to the end
I don't know what I'd do
If I found myself without you
So I'll say it once again
I am with you to the end
I love you all my friends
       -This is for my Friends

If it feels like your world is ending
Fear not
Everything must end
And although endings are sad
They are opportunities
For new beginnings
Fear not the end of your world
A new life awaits you
Born of fire
Born of ashes
Born of endings
        -Born of Endings

In all that I do
Wherever I go
Whatever I say
In all that I know
Love shall be the root
From which my future will grow
-Love Shall be the Root

To be human is to hurt
Is to cry
And is also to laugh
So maybe the reason you don't feel human
Isn't because you're hurting
Isn't because you're crying
It's because you're not laughing
   -To Be Human

We all have to take a leap of faith
At some point
And sometimes
We fall short
I can only hope
That someone is there
To grasp my hand
And bridge the gap
Of my shortcomings
      -Leap of Faith

Wretched things of troubled past,
Changed beyond repair and still,
Broken things that dare to last
Profane our worldly view until,
The broken thing is placed before us,
And daring to see beyond the cracks,
We find that broken things implore us,
To see its beauty still intact.
To see that all that has been lost
Pales compared to what is gained,
And find that grace's only cost
Is in the form of broken things.
   -Broken Things

What is the difference between a heart and a soul?
It's simple really
We use our heart for life
But we use our soul
To live
   -Heart and Soul

Drink!
Drink in life
Imbibe in it
Taste its sweetness
When life gives you lemons
Fucking eat them
Your life is your sustenance
So drink
Lest you drown in it
     -Drink

Slut shaming is
Utterly
Completely
Fucking
Stupid
It's your body
It's your life
Celebrate yourself
    -Slut Shaming

Age is naught but the passing of years
The tick tock of time and the dulling of fears
Or maybe they merely grow old with us too
From fears of the dark to when our mortgage is due

Or possibly age is the growth of our minds
Advancing from ignorance to one that's refined
A surge in our wisdom that makes us mature
As our views of the world are no longer pure

Or maybe age comes from the breaking of hearts
From the tragedy and sadness that tears us apart
From the ache and the pain that we all must endure
From the sickness of time for which there is no cure

Or perhaps age is growing weathered and old
As that fire in our eyes turns increasingly cold
As our hearts and our joints groan and complain
And every action becomes an endeavor of pain

But only after death the true test of age
Can really be known and really be gauged
The test is to see if our legacy lasts
If our lives are remembered or left in the past

To see if we've made a true change with our lives
Timeless legacies for which all humans strive
Comparable to Achilles or Arthur the King
Deeds about which future eras will sing
        -*The Nature of Age*

The End

A Word from the Author

Dear Reader,

Reaching this page means you're reached the end of my second poetry collection. Thank you so much for reading and supporting my work. Whether you've been following me since the beginning or this is your first time reading my poetry, I truly appreciate you taking the time to support me in my writing. If you enjoyed it, consider leaving a review on Amazon. I'd love to hear your feedback.

Sincerely,

-Travis Liebert

For more poetry by Travis Liebert:
Follow my Social Media:

Instagram - @travisliebert
Tumblr - @travisliebert
Facebook.com/authortravisliebert
Twitter - @travisliebert

Visit my website: alltheseinkspots.com

Find my other books on Amazon:

Perchance to Dream (Book 2 of *The Shattered Verses*)
Everything in Between (Book 3 of *The Shattered Verses*)
The Shattered Verses Collection

A Glimpse of
Perchance to Dream
(*The Shattered Verses* Book 2)

Angels wear their lipstick
On the corners of the street
Lined up for men to take their pick
Lined up like deli meats

I hear an old man shout
Howling about the world's end
I doubt the world is down and out
But it's surely done with him

It rains as cars pass by
All their lights are flashing
In solidarity the sky too cries
For a beloved person's passing

Trash floats down the alleyways
In a stream it twirls and spins
Along with it drifts my fate
Never to be seen again
            -Never To Be Seen

She is a woman
Like a million other women
Yet beautiful in her own way
She is a dandelion
That no one dares call a weed
   -Dandelion

I forgot to eat today
And by that
I mean
I "forgot" to eat today
I couldn't sleep last night either
My dreams kept me awake
Like a dream
That keeps you awake
You know?
It was jarring
Like an anti-simile
Like the first time
Your dad used a closed fist
Like reading your friend's name
In an obituary
Instead of the list
Of graduating students
        -*Jarring*

I have lived uncounted days
Resistant to the gaping grave
Resistant to all ill or plague
Lived to such breathtaking age
Ancient when the earth was formed
Older still when life was born
I watched you crawl upon the shore
Change and grow to something more
I gazed upon your petty wars
The woe and wounds and death you scored
Upon the enemies you scorned
I shall be old when you are done
Dead and swallowed by the sun
When every war's been lost or won
Time's ticking clock neglects to run
After millenia untold
When all the stars are weak and cold
As the universe begins to fold
I'll still be here, I'll still be old
                -Old

__About the Author__

Lauded as "a pretty nice guy," by his peers, Travis Liebert is a native of Louisville, Kentucky and a member of the widely invasive species "Homo sapiens sapiens." His hobbies include reading, writing, and anything else that indicates he's intelligent and literate. He went to Trinity High School where he openly brandished his stunning repertoire of useless knowledge as captain of the quick recall team. He is now a perpetually absent student at the University of Louisville. *Perchance to Dream* is his second poetry collection, following his first book *This is Death, Love, Life*. His third poetry collection, and the conclusion to *The Shattered Verses* series, is *Everything in Between*, which is currently available on Amazon.

Made in the USA
Columbia, SC
14 December 2019

84814351R00067